Royal Botanic Garden Edinburgh

G000152403

Text © Royal Botanic Garden Edinburgh, 2016

ISBN: 978-1-910877-13-5

Text by Sutherland Forsyth and edited by Donna Cole
Design/layout by Caroline Muir

The Royal Botanic Garden Edinburgh is a Non Departmental Public Body (NDPB) sponsored and supported through Grant-in-Aid by the Scottish Government's Environment and Forestry Directorate (ENFOR).

The Royal Botanic Garden Edinburgh is a Charity registered in Scotland (number SC007983).

All information correct at time of going to press.

Printed by Meigle Colour Printers Ltd

Foreword

Once in a generation a project comes along which captures the imagination: a project rich in history, full of uncertainty and risk, one where the odds are stacked against it but that if done right, can have a magnificent future. The Botanic Cottage is just such a project.

This handsome building is a testament to the Royal Botanic Garden Edinburgh's past, present and future.

Once standing at the entrance to a long-lost Georgian incarnation of the Garden, it served as a place of welcome, a home, and a classroom, and was a familiar sight for countless people during the height of the Scottish Enlightenment. From its design to its use, its owners to the illustrious names who were taught in it, the Botanic Cottage is now regarded as one of the best recorded small buildings in all of Scotland – a treasure trove of stories. This building also celebrates the achievements of the present: the tenacity of the campaigners who helped save it, the ingenuity of the team who worked out how to dismantle and move it across the city, the staff who found a new use for it, and the skills of all those who helped build it, making it look as good – if not better – than it did 250 years ago. Not only this, but as we look to the future, we do so with confidence and excitement that this special place will be enjoyed for many years to come, as people discover the wonders of nature in one of the great gardens of the world.

Rebuilt exactly 250 years to the day after it was first constructed in the 1760s, the Botanic Cottage has finally returned to its spiritual home.

Contents

Main cover image: Lynsey Wilson.
Lower back cover image: Stewart Attwood Photography.

The long-lost Leith Walk Botanic Garden

In 1760 King George III acceded to the throne, and the following year this young monarch began appointing a new generation of great men to important positions, many of whom lived and worked in Edinburgh: Robert Adam became Architect of the King's Works, Allan Ramsay was made Principal Painter in Ordinary, and John Hope became King's Botanist. Hope is the least well known, a largely forgotten luminary of the Scottish Enlightenment, but his contribution continues to be felt at the institution he transformed – the Royal Botanic Garden Edinburgh.

Founded by two pioneering Scottish doctors in 1670 on a small plot of land next to the Palace of Holyroodhouse, five years later the Botanic Garden had moved to the grounds of Trinity College Kirk and Hospital. As the decades passed, the collection of plants grew, and the importance of the Garden as a place to teach medical students about botany increased. The Regius Keeper – 'Chief Executive' – also served as the Professor of Botany and Materia Medica in the University. When Hope took over in 1761, he found an institution at a crossroads: there was no more space to expand, and there were frustrations with the quality of the land, risk of flooding, and the occasional invasions of sheep pushing down walls to get in to eat the plants! Something had to change, and Hope decided that the solution was to move lock, stock and barrel to a new site just under a mile away, on Leith Walk.

In 1763, Hope secured funding from the Crown to enable the move, making the most of the short premiership of the Earl of Bute, a Scot and a keen botanist. It was at this point that the Garden officially became known as the Royal Botanic Garden Edinburgh. It was one of the first major institutions to move to the north of the city, several years before the New Town was built. The five-acre plot was owned by Hope personally, and leased back to the State. His Principal Gardener, John Williamson, oversaw the major task of shifting plants from one garden to another, including some from the Royal Garden at Holyrood, also supervised by Hope.

The new garden was revolutionary, moving away from the rigid formality and largely medicinal focus of physic gardens, and instead, as a botanic garden, embracing all types of plants and their scientific value. It was unlike any other botanic garden at the time, with sweeping curved paths, mixing trees, shrubs and bedding plants, creating a great pond at the centre with a 140-foot glasshouse range overlooking it, and dispensary beds arranged according to the new classification system of Carl Linnaeus. The Garden became a popular place for visitors from both near and far, an institution of both beauty and botanical excellence.

At the entrance to the Leith Walk Botanic Garden there was a small but handsome building, familiar to everyone who passed along the street or visited the Garden, a building that would go on to have a remarkable story of its own – the Botanic Cottage.

Left: John Kay etching, 1786, depicting John Hope (left) in the Leith Walk Botanic Garden, talking to one of his gardeners. This is the only known image of Hope, who in addition to his positions as Regius Keeper and Professor of Botany, served as President of the Royal College of Physicians of Edinburgh and was a practising doctor with many patients in the city.

Right: Hope's 'To do' list from 1783.

Above: A street view of the Leith Walk Botanic Garden, painted by Jacob More in 1771. The Botanic Cottage is in the foreground, with the glasshouse range behind.

Below: A perspective view of the Leith Walk Garden by Jacob More from 1771, showing the garden as an oasis surrounded by fields, and the empty road that is now the bustling Leith Walk.

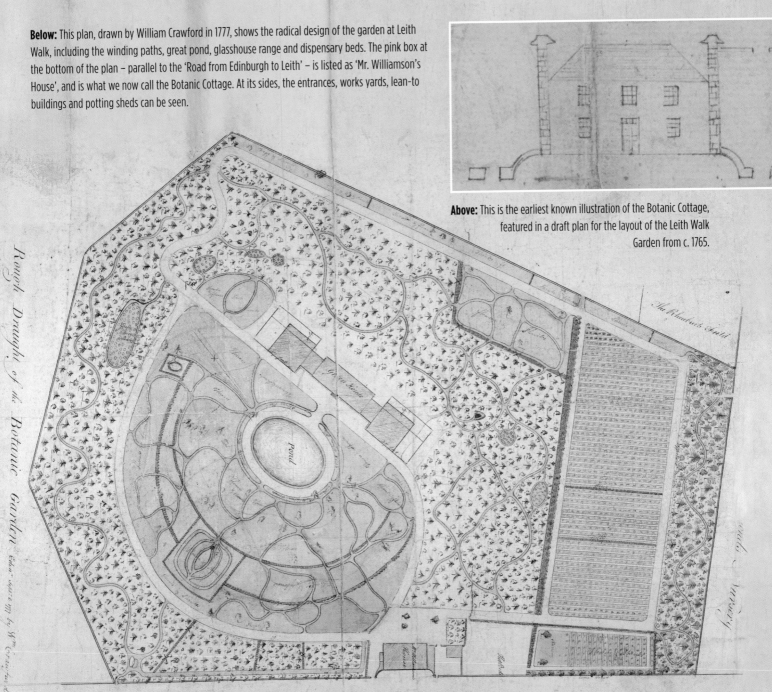

Below: This plan, drawn by William Crawford in 1777, shows the radical design of the garden at Leith Walk, including the winding paths, great pond, glasshouse range and dispensary beds. The pink box at the bottom of the plan – parallel to the 'Road from Edinburgh to Leith' – is listed as 'Mr. Williamson's House', and is what we now call the Botanic Cottage. At its sides, the entrances, works yards, lean-to buildings and potting sheds can be seen.

Above: This is the earliest known illustration of the Botanic Cottage, featured in a draft plan for the layout of the Leith Walk Garden from c. 1765.

Rough Draught of the Botanic Garden

pond

Road from Edinburgh to Leith

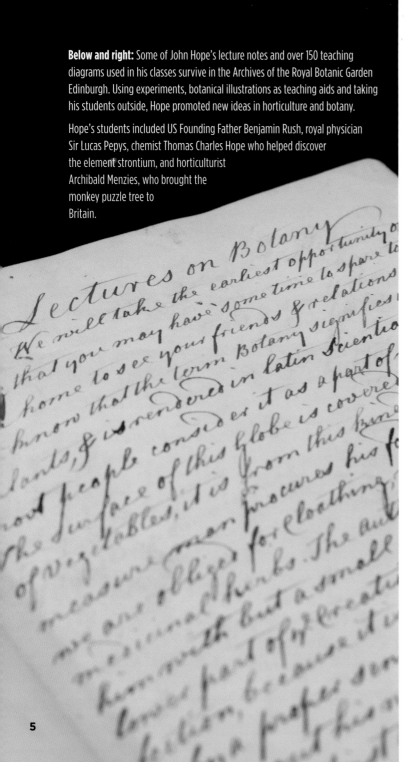

A home, a classroom, a place of welcome

In 1764, John Hope commissioned his old school friend, John Adam, to design a building to stand at the entrance of his newly created garden, which became known as the Botanic Cottage. Adam, brother of Robert and a key player in the family architectural business, may well have worked with a young apprentice by the name of James Craig, who soon after went on to gain fame by designing the plan for the Edinburgh New Town.

The building was to have three purposes: the ground floor would provide accommodation for the Principal Gardener and his family, initially John Williamson, his wife and three children; the wing walls and doors at either side of the house would serve as staff and public entrances to the Garden; and the upstairs would be a classroom and work space for Hope, where medical students could be taught botany each May, June and July.

Built of Craigleith-type sandstone, some of which may have been recycled from other buildings, it took just over a year to build. Although the main building work was finished at the end of 1765, archival evidence shows that some elements were still being completed the following year.

Nº III

Nº IIII

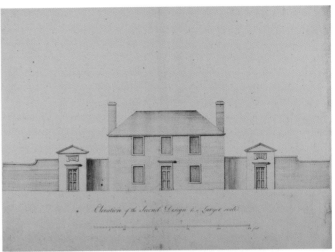

Elevation of the Second Design to a Larger scale

Fig 1   Fig 2   Fig 3   Fig 4

Fig 5   Fig 6

Fig 7

Fig 8   Fig 9   Fig 10

Fig 11   Fig 12

I

Gentlemen

The word Botany is derived from the Greek & comes from ΒΟΤΑΝΥ signifying a plant. It may be taken in two senses, 1st for the knowledge of plants 2nd for the knowledge of all & every thing that relates to them as vegetation their structure &c. Before we begin we shall lay before you the plan of this intended course in order that you may know what you are to expect from it & that you may connect together the different parts of it. We are indebted to the vegetable kingdom for our food (Drink included) cloathing & for most of the necessaries as well as the ornaments of life. Man differs from other animals in this that he has very little instinct from which the other animals derive their knowledge & as he has not this he must have recourse to other means in order to become acquainted with the nature & properties of vegetables, & this he does by the application of his senses & a judicious induction.

6

BOTANIC GARDEN

WHEREAS much inconvenience has arisen from the crowds of of promiscuous company walking in the Botanic Garden, by which the necessary work has been interrupted, and proper distinction of visitors could not be made,

On these and other accounts, it has become necessary to admit none, without an order from the Professor of Botany.

By this regulation it is not meant to render access to the Garden difficult: Strangers, the Gentlemen of this country, the Citizens of Edinburgh, and any person of knowledge or curiosity, upon sending their name to the shops of

Mr Thomson druggist, head of Niddry's Wynd,

Mr Spankie, opposite to the Tron Church,

Mr Moncrieff apothecary, on the Bridge,

will receive an order for seeing the Garden, between the hours of twelve and three, and during the summer at six in the evening, every day, Sunday excepted.

Left and below: Such was the popularity of the Garden with both academics and public alike, that in 1782 a notice had to be placed in the *Edinburgh Evening Courant* advising that a ticketing system was being introduced to control the numbers of visitors. It is notable, however, that there is no mention of a charge for the tickets, and ultimately the only qualification that one needed to enter the Garden was 'curiosity'.

All visitors, whoever they were, would have entered through the doors on either side of the Botanic Cottage – and students and staff would have walked through the front door.

The Edinburgh Evening Courant

MAY 4. 1782.

(No. 10,031) — SATURDAY,

Printed for FLEMING AND RAMSAY, in the OLD FISH-MARKET CLOSE.

THEATRE-ROYAL.

FOR THE BENEFIT OF

MR. TAYLOR AND MRS. KNIVETON,

WEDNESDAY EVENING, the 8th of May, will be presented

THE COMEDY OF

A TRIP TO SCARBOROUGH.

Lord Foppington, Mr WARD,
...shion, Mr Williamson—Colonel Townly, Mr Knight—Probe,
...nson—La Varole, Mr Marshall—Sir Tunbelly Clumsey, Mr
...sworth—Lory, Mr Hallion—Hosier, Mr Simpson—Taylor,
...arteris—Shoemaker, Mr T. Banks,
And Lovelefs, Mr WOODS.
Amanda, Mrs WARD,
Mifs Kirby—Nurfe, Mrs Charteris—Mrs Coupler, MrsMount-
fort—Sempftress, Mrs Henderson,
And Mifs Hoyden, Mrs KNIVETON.
Preceding the Play,
...ertation on *Every Body, Some Body, and No Body,*
BY MR TAYLOR.
...the Play and Farce, a Pantomimical Interlude, called
PAUL JONES IN THE FRITH,
OR LEITH IN AN UPROAR.
...'Intoſh, Mr Charteris—M'Nab, Mr Simpson—M'Dulcan,
...aylor—Regulating Captain (with a Song), Mr Marshall,
Lucky Peacock, Mr Hollingsworth,
...quin (in the Character of Paul Jones)—Mr T. BANKS,
...ill make his escape from the BATTERY by jumping thro'
A HOGSHEAD ON FIRE.
To which will be added, by Defire,

IRISH STATE LOTTERY 1782.

Not two Blanks to a Prize, and the Prizes to be paid in full in Irish currency.
THE TICKETS AND SHARES OF TICKETS,
From a Half to a Sixteenth, either on the usual mode, or on a plan of returning Ten Pounds for each blank, are sold and registered by

WHITE AND MITCHELL,

At their Toy Shop and State Lottery-Office, opposite to the Tron Church, EDINBURGH,

Agents for Meſſ. RICHARDSON and GOODLUCK, London,

(Remarkable for selling the moſt capital prizes.)

ALSO,

CAPITAL CHANCES, containing twenty different numbers, at Two GUINEAS, ONE GUINEA, and HALF-A-GUINEA each.

Schemes of the Lottery, which begins drawing the 24th June, with particulars of the above plans, to be had *gratis* at the office.

Letters poſt paid duly answered, and money at *current rate* for the *prizes* in former lotteries.

SALE OF PRIZE GOODS.

To be SOLD by public auction, in different Lots, at the Warehouse of Meſſrs. RAMSAY, WILLIAMSON, AND Co. Leith, on Monday the 20th of May current, precisely at ten o'clock forenoon,

THE following GOODS, being part of the Cargo of the ſnow FOUR FRIENDS (prize to the LIVELY PRIVATEER, Willis Machell commander), taken on her paſſage from Amsterdam to Boston,—viz.

106 Pieces fine broad cloth.	24 Turkey leather pocket-books.
40 Pieces flannel and duffle.	96 Pair silk garters.
5 Pieces caſſimere.	30 Umbrellas.
60 Dozen pair of ſtockings.	22 Reams of paper.
100 Pieces ſhalloon, poplin, denin,	Pair of womens shoes.

Carron Grates, Light Kitchen Furnit...

To be Sold on the Loweſt Terms,

At W. BRAIDWOOD'S Carron Warehouſe, near Heriot... market, Edinburgh,

A LARGE and Elegant Aſſortment of CARRON G... fitted up to all the common ſizes, and a great var... anſwer chimnies of any ſize whatever—Smoke Stoves... ſtruction with Brodie's Regiſter Fire Stoves, made to c... Grates, ſo conſtructed as to admit of their ſtanding in... of the form of Steel Grates, with pillars and vaſes— Boiling Tables, Pedeſtal Stoves, Laundry Heater and... Furnace Doors and Grates, Pots, Kettles, ſmoothing... ſorts of Carron Goods.

A very fine aſſortment of Engliſh Cut Fenders, F... ribbed Fenders, tinned Iron Spoons, Coal Backets a... lows, Jacks, Frying Pans, Branders, &c.—Alſo a pa... ſicks, to be ſold very cheap in wholeſale.

Light Annealed Caſt Iron Goblets and Stew Pa... Carron, equal in quality to the patent Engliſh pans, ar... which reduces theſe valuable articles to one half o... beſides ſaving the enormous expence of tinning, wh... ſort has no occaſion ever to be renewed.—Light... much improved, the bodies and ſpouts being caſt i... renders them more durable than the Engliſh ones.— Engliſh Pots of all ſizes.

Geography, Mathematics, and N...

ROBERT DARLING is juſt beginning a cour... the uſe of the Globes, in Geography and A... ſecond land above the Exchange, Edinburgh, whe... taught to do all the problems particularly on the G...

He alſo teaches Navigation for young gentlemen... alſo Fortification and Gunnery, &c. Land-ſurveyin...

Tragedy struck the Garden on 23 September 1780. In addition to being Principal Gardener, John Williamson also worked part-time as a customs officer. That morning he heard that some smugglers had made their way up from the port in Leith to the recently built Princes Street, and he decided to seek them out. However, when he located the smugglers, they turned on him and he was beaten to death.

The murder of a respected and familiar face sent shockwaves through the city, but the criminals were never found. John Hope commissioned James Craig to design a memorial to Williamson, with the intention of placing it above the entrance to the Garden at the side of the Botanic Cottage; enhancements to the facade of the cottage may also have been made at this time.

Seven Principal Gardeners lived in the Botanic Cottage: John Williamson, Malcolm McCoig (depicted speaking to Hope in John Kay's illustration on page 1), Robert Menzies, John Mackay, George Don, Thomas Sommerville and William McNab.

Sommerville died suddenly at the age of 27 after only three years in the role, and a sale of his personal collection of books and curiosities was held in the Botanic Cottage in April 1810. This document not only gives an insight into the man, his interests and his thirst for knowledge, but also gives a sense of some of the items that would have filled the rooms of the Cottage.

Below: The Williamson memorial and a page from the Sommerville auction catalogue.

6.

135 Wigeon, stuffed
Golden Pheasant, ditto
Pressing Boards, Papers, &c. with a number of dried Specimens of plants
Book for collecting dried Specimens
Ebony Inkstand, with Rulers, &c.
140 Sharping-stone, in Mahogany case
Withering's Botany, 4 vols, 8vo.   Lond. 1801
Lightfoot's Flora Scotica,   -   ib. 1777
Ditto,   -   -   -   -   - ib. 1792
Linnæi Systema Naturæ,   -   Lugd. 1756
145 Sir Thomas More's Flower Garden dis-
played, 4to.   -   -   - Lond. 1734
Willdinow's Linnæi Species Plantarum,
3 vols. 8vo. bound in six parts, Berolini, 1797
Linnæi Musa Cliffortiana, 4to,   Lugd. 1736
Boerhaave's Index Plantarum,   ib. 1710
Linnæus's System of Nature, 7 vols. trans-
lated by Turton, 8vo.   -   Lond. 1806
150 Hall's British Flora, vol. 1.   Manch. 1808
Smith's Flora Britannica, 3 vols. 8vo. Lond. 1800
——'s Compendium Floræ Britannicæ, ib. 1800
Aiton's Hortus Kewensis, 3 vols. 8vo. ib. 1789
Don's Hortus Cantabrigiensis,   Camb. 1807
155 Liverpool Catalogue of Plants,   Liverp. 1808
Hudson's Flora Anglica,   -   Lond. 1798
Zarda Pharmaca Vegetabilia,   Prague, 1792
Dickson's Catalogue of Plants, and two
others,   -   -   -   Edin. 1794
Mentzelius Index Plantarum, fol. Berolini, 1682

Below: Throughout the 19th and 20th centuries almost the entire site of the Leith Walk Botanic Garden was built over.

Life after the Botanics

By 1820, over 4,000 species of plant were growing in the Botanic Garden. With increased development around Leith Walk, there was a need to find a new, larger site for the Garden. Several options were investigated, but a 14-acre plot in Inverleith was chosen by Regius Keeper Robert Graham, and over the next three years each plant was moved across the city. One of the last elements to be brought to the new Garden was the memorial to John Williamson, taken off the front of the Botanic Cottage and inscribed to mark the occasion of its move.

The days of the Leith Walk incarnation of the Royal Botanic Garden Edinburgh were over, but the next chapter in the life of the Botanic Cottage was only just beginning.

Since the mid-17th century, Leith Walk had been a road on two levels – a lower track on the western side running past the Garden, and on the eastern side, 3 metres higher, stood a raised causeway, built when Edinburgh was occupied by Oliver Cromwell's forces. After the Garden left the site, the street level on the western side was brought up to match its eastern neighbour, completely covering the old walls of the Garden, and obscuring the ground floor of the Botanic Cottage. As the 19th century progressed, the

Above: Only the upper storey was visible from Leith Walk after the street level was raised.

lime render was either washed away or deliberately removed, possibly influenced by the Victorian taste for exposed rather than rendered stone. In 1849, the building was formally listed on an Ordnance Survey map as the 'Botanic Cottage'. It suffered a further indignity in 1911 when a tenement was built beside it, requiring approximately 3 feet of the west gable wall to be removed in order to finish this new block of flats.

Despite now being half hidden, no longer having a smart render finish and having lost one end wall, the Cottage continued to be occupied. It had become a private home, often tied to a large plot of land behind it that once contained part of the Garden, the rest having been built over. However, in the early 20th century this site became the base for the building merchant David Y. Abbey, with the Cottage serving as a house for the

foreman. In the 1960s, a monumental mason with the nickname of 'Tappy Frank' (as the residents always heard him tapping away at stones with his chisel), occupied a small space in front of the Cottage, between the raised street level and the building. By this time only the upstairs was used as a home, the ground floor having become storage.

Left: The Cottage in the early 1990s, after the new walkway had been built and a front door installed where a window had been.

Below: In 2007 the Cottage was a sorry state – fire damaged, abandoned and set for demolition.

A garage was built beside the Cottage in the 1970s, the building merchants having now left, and by the late 1980s the Cottage itself changed from residential use and became the office of a chartered surveyor. The following decade saw yet more change, with a raised walkway leading from the street level of Leith Walk, providing access to a newly created front door made out of the central upstairs window. A van rental shop moved in, becoming a familiar place to many people living in Edinburgh who remember popping into what they thought was a funny little building to hire a vehicle. After this company moved on, the Cottage was abandoned in the early 2000s, and it and the site behind were sold for redevelopment.

In 2007 it was set on fire and only saved from total destruction by people spotting the smoke and raising the alarm. Word got out that the Cottage was to be demolished, and a hotel built on the site. With no listed building status, there appeared to be little hope.

Below: The rear of the Botanic Cottage in the mid-20th century, by which time numerous alterations had been made to this Georgian house. The turret contained a stairwell which was added in 1802 to give more space inside the building.

Below: Rubble sits in the nursery of the Botanics, awaiting rebuilding.

Saving the Botanic Cottage

In the spring of 2007, a few local residents heard that the Cottage was set to be demolished, and spread the word through the Friends of Hopetoun Crescent Garden (situated in a small fragment in the north-west corner of the original Leith Walk Garden) and at public meetings. 'Could something be done?' they asked, but with no listed building status and little information about its history, the answer appeared to be 'No'. Undeterred, a coalition of interested parties began to form: neighbours, architects, historians, researchers, volunteers, horticulturists and more. A meeting was convened at the Royal Botanic Garden Edinburgh, at the invitation of the then Regius Keeper Stephen Blackmore.

It was concluded that the best that could probably be hoped for was to undertake a detailed study of the building, ensuring that a record would survive even if the Cottage did not. However, renowned conservation architect James Simpson did note at that meeting that, in exceptional circumstances, it is possible to move buildings. Little did the attendees realise just how exceptional the Botanic Cottage would turn out to be.

With a grant from the Heritage Lottery Fund, stewarded by the Friends of Hopetoun Crescent Garden, with support from the Alba Conservation Trust, research began, involving a range of interested parties and individuals. They uncovered a wealth of information: the original receipts for tradesmen who supplied materials and labour, historic drawings and paintings of the building kept in the RBGE Archives, the names of over 1,000 students taught in the historic classroom, and the original teaching diagrams and lecture notes. Indeed, it turned out that the building, now known to have been designed by two of the most noted architects of the Georgian era, contained the only classroom to survive from the height of the Scottish Enlightenment (Edinburgh's original college buildings having been knocked down in the late 18th century). Day after day, new discoveries were made, to the point that by the early summer that year the research team were of the view that the Cottage was one of the best recorded small buildings in all of Scotland. Yet it was still set to be knocked down.

Fortunately, the developer who now owned the site became convinced of the importance of the Cottage, and the idea that it could perhaps be moved began to be discussed further. In a generous gesture, the demolition contractor offered to dismantle the building, numbering the key stones, quoin stones and even timbers, free of charge. The opportunity to bring the Cottage 'home', to the current incarnation of the Royal Botanic Garden Edinburgh, and to be rebuilt by the same institution that had originally commissioned it, could not be passed up.

Below and right: Even a list of food from 1777 was found.

Above: Fretwork panels tell the story of saving the Botanic Cottage.

The Botanic Cottage Trust was formed, chaired by a distant kinsman of John Hope, Lord Hope of Craighead, to oversee this important phase. In 2008, work began to take the building apart, with careful assessment by archaeologists from University of Glasgow and Addyman Archaeology. The Trust took legal ownership of the stones and timbers in 2008, which were placed onto pallets and transported across Edinburgh to the nursery of the Botanic Gardens. The Trust later passed ownership to Royal Botanic Garden Edinburgh.

A new vision for the future of the Botanic Cottage was formed. Inspired by its original use, it would be rebuilt as a community and education hub for the Garden, providing much needed spaces for teaching, shelter, cooking and much more, just a stone's throw from the school, student and community plots located in the area behind the magnificent beech hedge. Architects Simpson & Brown were employed to work out how to rebuild the Cottage so that it looked as good as it did in its Georgian heyday, but also so that it was fit for the 21st century. Additional rooms were created on the site of the original potting sheds and works yards, whilst a lift to the upper room, storage and, of course, toilets, were all able to be included in the rebuilt cottage.

Above: Rubble sits in the nursery.
Below: Numbered timbers and stones awaiting rebuilding.

Digging deeper

During the rebuilding of the Botanic Cottage, archaeologists undertook excavations of the old site at Leith Walk, uncovering new information about the building and the long-lost garden.

Led by experts from Addyman Archaeology, a team of volunteers assisted the dig of the Cottage site, gently clearing away layers of dirt to reveal the foundations of the building. They helped to record the area in meticulous detail and found what is thought to have been the masonry footings of a timber staircase that might have provided access to the upstairs of the building before the turnpike stair was added in 1802. Furthermore, a volunteer found that the area in front of the ground floor of the Cottage had once been covered in rounded cobble stones.

In this and the wider digs of the land behind the Cottage, archaeologists found a range of fascinating items: fragments of Georgian plates and a figurine, an early 19th-century child's shoe, a moulded clay pipe, copious amounts of broken terracotta plant pots, a button featuring the royal coat of arms and much more. Not only this, but the team even found the remains of a path that corresponded with a garden plan from 1777, drainage systems, a barrel of lime, the base of what may well have been a sundial or other garden ornament, and the outline of plant beds.

Left: Volunteers worked with archaeologists to investigate the foundations of the Botanic Cottage.

Above: A Georgian figurine, an early 19th-century shoe, and one of many fragments of china found on the digs.

Above: The thin cream line is the base of one of the original Leith Walk Botanic Garden paths as seen in cross section.

Above: Twenty volunteers supported the excavation of the foundations of the Botanic Cottage over the course of eight days.

Rebuilding the Botanic Cottage

After six years of planning, designing and fundraising, work began on the rebuilding of the Botanic Cottage in September 2014. A competitive tender process saw Maxi Construction appointed as the main contractor, with a number of trade sub-contractors, executing work under the direction of the architects Simpson & Brown.

The Cottage was to be rebuilt to match the 18th-century drawings, incorporating all of the salvaged materials including numbered stones, timbers and rubble. Where additional materials were required, these were sourced to match the originals.

The process of rebuilding saw work undertaken almost exactly 250 years to the day after it was originally done, right down to some contractors working on identical projects on the very same dates. Indeed, the team can claim to be the only people alive to have built a Georgian house from scratch, with two-feet-thick walls, roofed and finished externally and internally in the traditional way.

Left: Rebuilding the stone staircase, with the old handrail back in place at the top.

Right: Green energy features in the rebuilt Cottage include solar and photovoltaic panels and an air source heat pump. These help to provide electricity, hot water and contribute to the underfloor heating of the building.

Above and below: The masons used all the original stones set with hot lime mortar for the two-feet-thick solid walls. For the missing west end wall, removed when a tenement was built against the Cottage in 1911, the stone rubble was generously provided by the new owners of the Leith Walk site from part of the old garden wall that had survived below street level.

Two apprentices worked alongside the stonemasons during the project, providing them with hands-on experience of cutting, carving and laying stones. Additional stone, required for the front wing walls and for repairing missing or damaged stones, came from the Hazeldean quarry in Northumberland, the closest match for the Craigleith-type sandstone used in the historic Cottage walls.

Above and left: Behind the side-wing walls there would have been works yards, potting sheds, lean-to buildings and courtyards, as well as doorways providing entrances into the old Leith Walk Garden. These had largely been lost, and so new wing walls were constructed. Behind them, the architects created new teaching spaces and facilities, following the approximate footprint of the old yards and buildings (based on surviving plans in the RBGE archives). These were built using red brick and pan tiles, which were found to be the materials used for garden outbuildings during the archaeology digs of the Leith Walk site. To support the side-wing roofs, pillars were cut from a chestnut tree felled in the Botanic Garden in 2013.

Below: In order to get an authentic finish on the historic interior walls, approximately 5,000 strips of oak lath were individually nailed to the walls (insulated with sheep's wool), before three layers of lime plaster were smoothed on top.

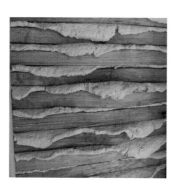

Above and right: An information shed was visited by over 14,000 people during the rebuilding, a further 3,000 people attended events about the Cottage, and 7,000 people used resources created including trails, information cards and short films.

Alongside the rebuilding of the Cottage, there was an extensive programme of public engagement, with events, talks, tours, displays and publications, which helped thousands of people to discover the story of this remarkable building. The public was kept up to date with the progress of the build through social media, from the moment of breaking ground until the day of opening.

Step inside the Botanic Cottage

Exactly 250 years after the first students were taught in the Botanic Cottage in May of 1766, it reopened as a centre for education and community engagement. From the large Potting Shed in the east wing to the light and bright Garden Room in the west, the Kitchen in the heart of the building to the historic Professor's Room – the original Enlightenment classroom – these wonderful spaces provide a unique venue for people of all ages and backgrounds to discover the world of plants, take part in health and wellbeing activities, learn to cook or do art, and so much more.

Rebuilt with love and integrity, the Botanic Cottage is a building to be proud of: proud of its past, proud of its present and proud of its future. Important architecturally and historically, it now once again stands in its spiritual home, ready to be enjoyed for generations to come.

Left: Inside the Professor's Room, where Professor John Hope taught botany to medical students. Replicas of his teaching diagrams hang on the walls.

Above: With its lime render finish and medicinal plants in front, the completed Botanic Cottage is a handsome addition to the Garden.

Above: The Kitchen.

Above: The Kitchen dresser.

Above: The turnpike staircase.

Above: Entering the Professor's Room.

Above: Once again, people will be able to be informed and inspired in this historic classroom.

Above: The Garden Room sits behind the west wing wall.

Above: Inside the Potting Shed.

Royal
Botanic Garden
Edinburgh

Acknowledgements

Rebuilding the Botanic Cottage would not have been possible without the support of
many generous trusts, foundations and individuals, in particular the Heritage Lottery Fund.
The Royal Botanic Garden Edinburgh is incredibly grateful for their generosity.

The extensive research undertaken by Jane Corrie and Joe Rock, along with the work of Henry Noltie,
James Simpson, Leonie Paterson and many other individuals, made this book possible.

Thank you

The Royal Botanic Garden Edinburgh thanks the following individuals and organisations
who supported the rebuilding of the Botanic Cottage:

Heritage Lottery Fund Scotland

Friends, Companions and Patrons of
the Royal Botanic Garden Edinburgh

The Binks Trust

Magdalene Sharp Erskine
Dunimarle Trust

The Robertson Trust

The Wolfson Foundation

Dunard Fund

EDF Energy Green Fund

The Gannochy Trust

Garfield Weston Foundation

The MacRobert Trust

Wellcome Trust

Cruden Foundation

Edina Trust

The Ernest Cook Trust

The Nancie Massey Charitable Trust

The Steel Charitable Trust

The Thistledown Trust

The Best Trust

Alan Evans Memorial Trust

Dalrymple Donaldson Fund

The Gunter Charitable Trust

The Janelaw Trust

Sir James Miller Edinburgh Trust

Sir Ewan and Lady Brown

Nicola Ferguson

Dr Henry Noltie

Mary Robertson

Ian and Flora Sword

Zachs-Adams Family

The Botanic Cottage Trust

Simpson and Brown Architects

And many individual and
anonymous donors